FACES

written by **SHELLEY ROTNER** and **KEN KREISLER**
photographs by **SHELLEY ROTNER**

HOUGHTON MIFFLIN COMPANY
BOSTON
ATLANTA   DALLAS   GENEVA, ILLINOIS   PALO ALTO   PRINCETON

1999 Impression
Houghton Mifflin Edition, 1996

Printed in the U.S.A.

ISBN: 0-395-75256-6

9-B-99

In memory of my grandmother—
a face I will always remember.
—S. R.

For Samantha
—K. K.

Faces, faces, all kinds of faces.

Faces talking,

faces smelling,

faces hearing,

faces seeing.

Thinking faces,

sleeping faces,

friendly faces,

faces feeling.

Funny faces

sometimes masked,

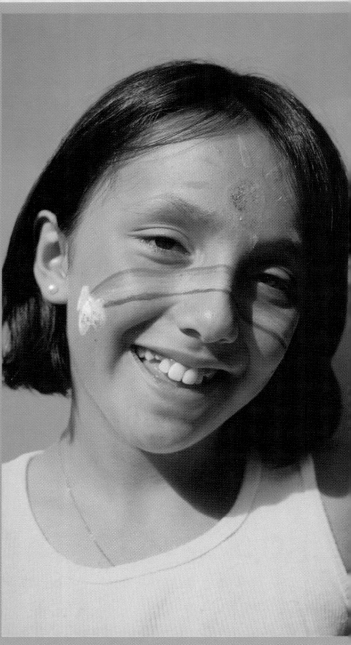

sometimes painted.

 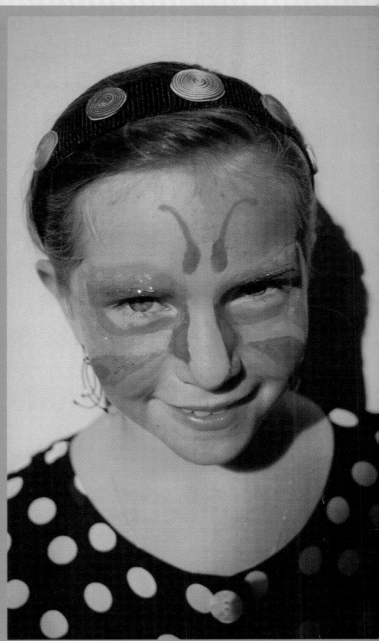

All different,

21

each special in its own way.

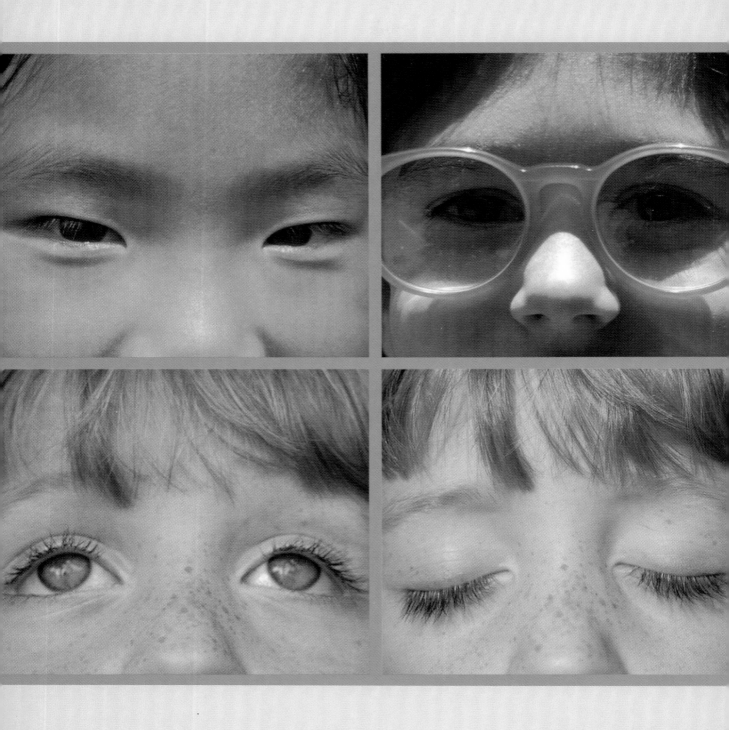

Eyes,

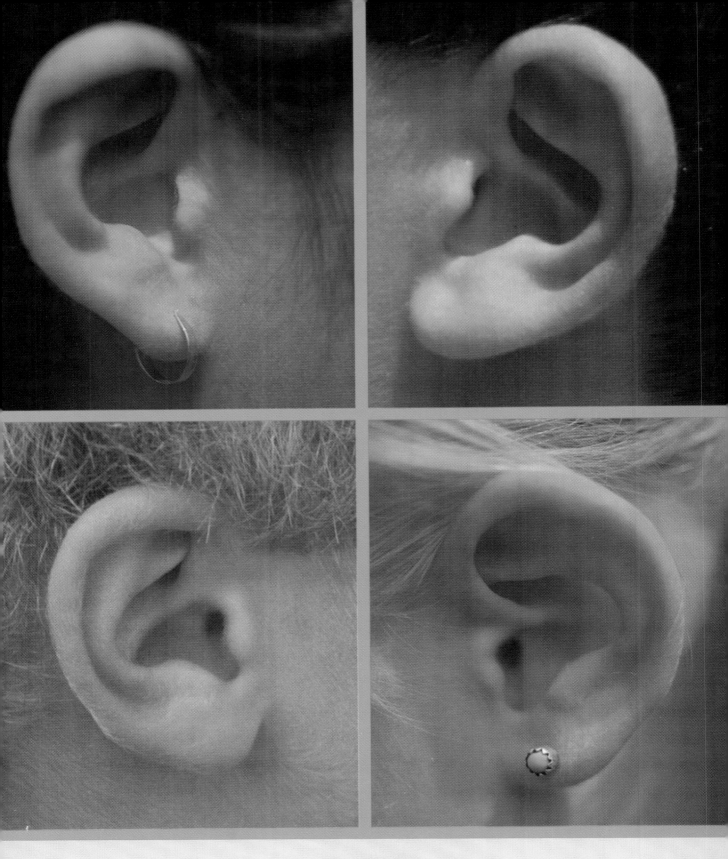

ears.

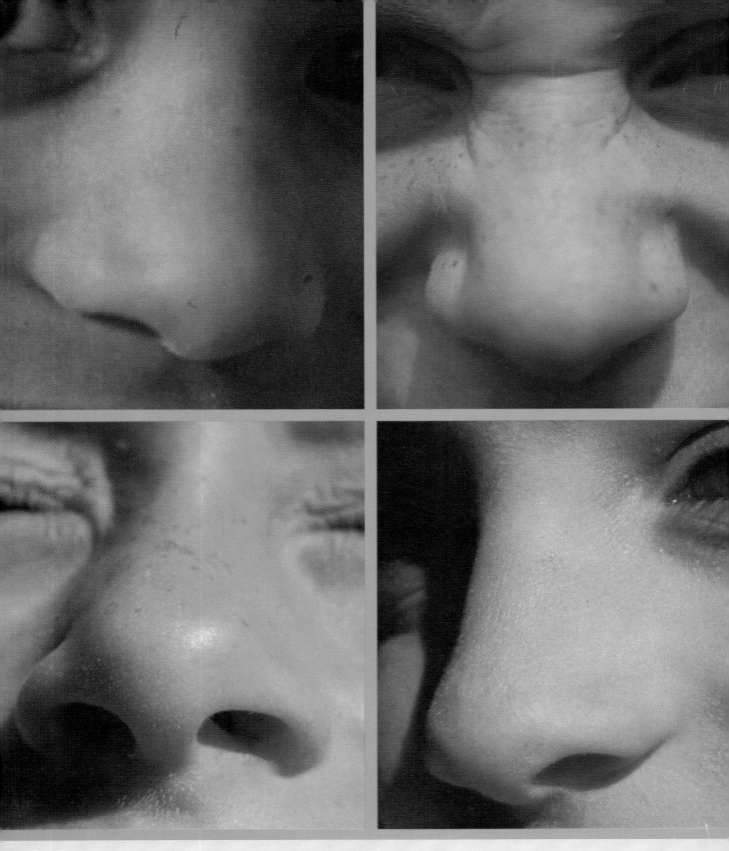

Noses,

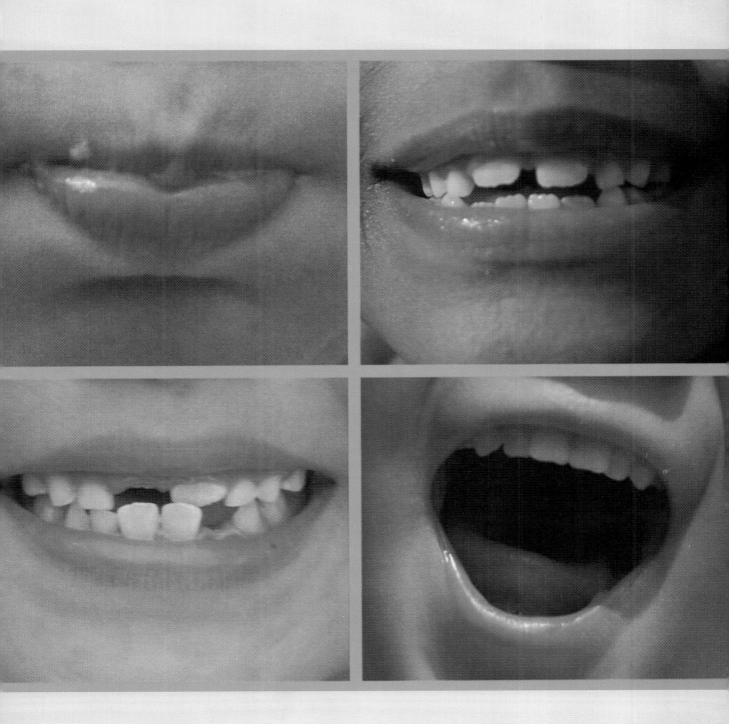

mouths.

Faces, faces, from all kinds of places.

Faces.